Contents

All About Animals

Many millions of different kinds, or species, of animals live on Earth. The scientists who study living things have divided those they know into different groups. All the animals that belong to each group have something in common. For example, they may all have no backbone or their skeletons may be outside their bodies. Some groups are so large that they have to be divided again into smaller groups.

Mollusks

Mollusks are soft-bodied animals that usually live in water. Mollusks include snails, oysters, and other shellfish that have a hard, outer shell, as well as octopuses, squid, and slugs.

Animals with Backbones

The vertebrates are the group of animals that have backbones and skeletons inside their bodies. The five main groups are fish, amphibians, reptiles, birds, and mammals, including human beings.

Amphibians

Amphibians are animals that can live both in water and on land. The word amphibian comes from a Greek word that means "leading a double life." Frogs, toads, salamanders, newts, and caecilians are all amphibians.

Fish

Fish make up the largest vertebrate group. Some live in fresh water, others in the sea. Fish such as trout and salmon are called bony fish. Sharks have gristle for skeletons, not bone. They are called cartilaginous fish.

Reptiles

Turtles, crocodiles, snakes, and lizards are all reptiles. Most live on land, although a few reptiles, such as turtles and marine iguanas, live in the sea.

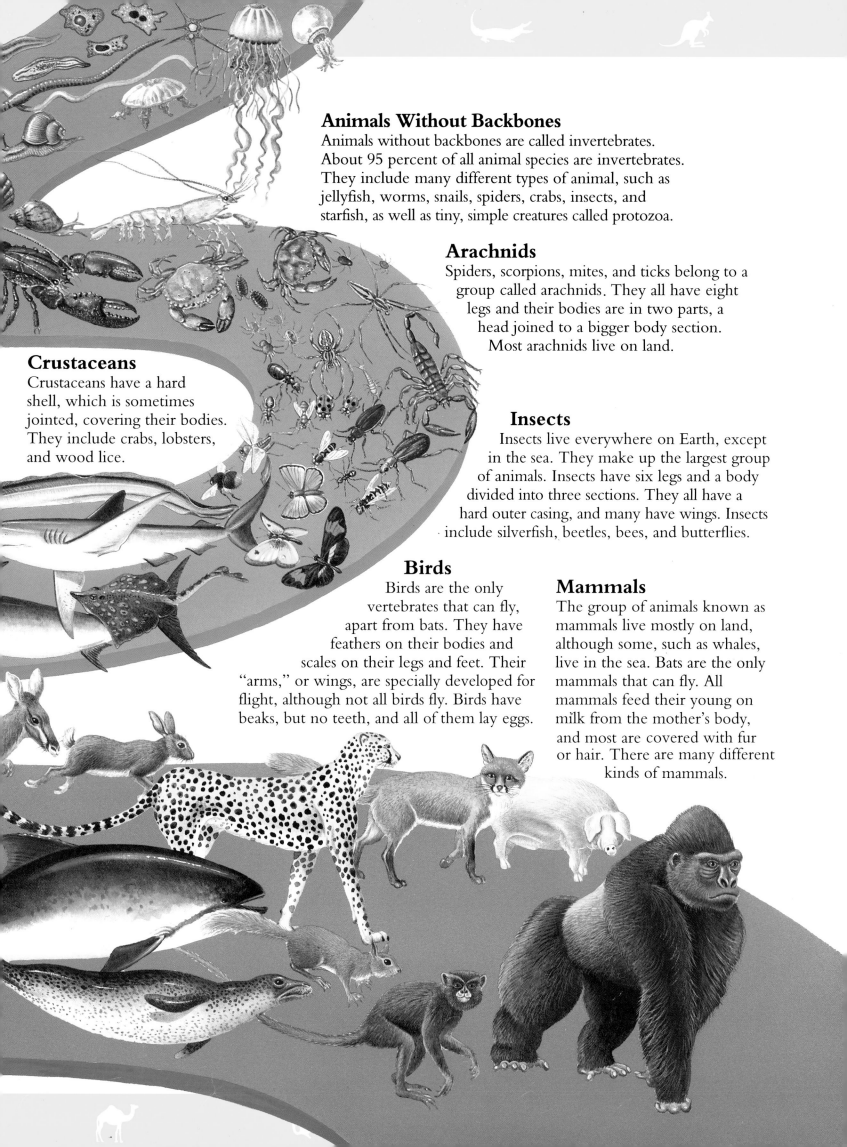

Animals Without Backbones

Animals without backbones are called invertebrates. About 95 percent of all animal species are invertebrates. They include many different types of animal, such as jellyfish, worms, snails, spiders, crabs, insects, and starfish, as well as tiny, simple creatures called protozoa.

Arachnids

Spiders, scorpions, mites, and ticks belong to a group called arachnids. They all have eight legs and their bodies are in two parts, a head joined to a bigger body section. Most arachnids live on land.

Crustaceans

Crustaceans have a hard shell, which is sometimes jointed, covering their bodies. They include crabs, lobsters, and wood lice.

Insects

Insects live everywhere on Earth, except in the sea. They make up the largest group of animals. Insects have six legs and a body divided into three sections. They all have a hard outer casing, and many have wings. Insects include silverfish, beetles, bees, and butterflies.

Birds

Birds are the only vertebrates that can fly, apart from bats. They have feathers on their bodies and scales on their legs and feet. Their "arms," or wings, are specially developed for flight, although not all birds fly. Birds have beaks, but no teeth, and all of them lay eggs.

Mammals

The group of animals known as mammals live mostly on land, although some, such as whales, live in the sea. Bats are the only mammals that can fly. All mammals feed their young on milk from the mother's body, and most are covered with fur or hair. There are many different kinds of mammals.

All About Vertebrates

The animals that have a long backbone, made up of a row of small bones joined together, are known as vertebrates. The small bones are called vertebrae, which is where the name "vertebrate" comes from. Each vertebrate has a hard skeleton inside it that supports and protects its soft body. The delicate brain is kept safe from harm inside a bony case, the skull.

There are five main groups of vertebrates – fish, amphibians, reptiles, birds, and mammals. The animals covered in this book are all land-living vertebrates from the amphibian, reptile, and mammal groups.

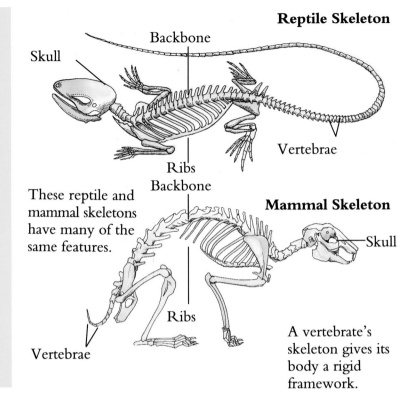

Reptile Skeleton

Skull

Backbone

Vertebrae

Ribs

These reptile and mammal skeletons have many of the same features.

Backbone

Mammal Skeleton

Skull

Ribs

Vertebrae

A vertebrate's skeleton gives its body a rigid framework.

Amphibians

Amphibians can live both in water and on land. They are cold-blooded, which means that their body temperature is the same as their surroundings. Many amphibians begin life as tiny, fishlike tadpoles that live in water and breathe through gills. As they grow, their bodies slowly change. By the time they are adults, they are able to live on land and breathe air through lungs. The 4,000 or so species of amphibians are divided into three groups – frogs and toads, newts and salamanders, and caecilians.

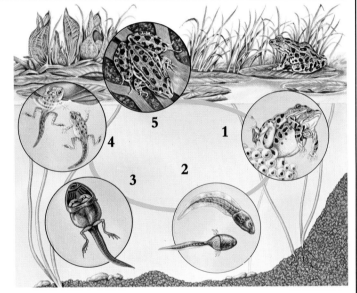

Frogs have smooth skins and are usually smaller and slimmer than toads.

Frog

Frogs can breathe through their skin, as well as through their lungs.

Webbed toes and strong back legs make frogs good swimmers.

Newts "walk" by wriggling from side to side and pushing forward with their feet.

Frogs lay their eggs in water (1). The eggs hatch out into tadpoles (2). The tadpoles slowly change into adults (3 and 4), then come out of water to breathe air and live on land (5).

Blind, wormlike caecilians live underground in hot countries.

Newt

Caecilian

Reptiles

Nearly all reptiles live on land and breathe air. They have scaly, waterproof skin that keeps them from losing moisture. This makes them well suited to living in dry climates.

Like amphibians, reptiles are cold-blooded. Most of them lay eggs, which usually have soft, leathery shells.

Except for alligators and crocodiles, most reptiles are fairly small. There are about 6,500 species of reptile, divided into four groups - alligators and crocodiles, tortoises and turtles, snakes and lizards, and one reptile, the tuatara, which is a type on its own.

Turtle

Tortoises and turtles are protected from enemies by their strong shells.

The backbone of a snake may have up to 400 vertebrae.

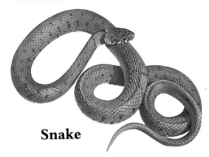

Snake

Crocodile

The largest reptiles, crocodiles and alligators, are meat-eaters.

A young crocodile has a thickened patch of skin on the end of its nose to help it break its shell.

Mammals

Mammals are warm-blooded animals. This means that their blood temperature stays the same, even in very cold or hot weather. Most mammals have fur or hair. They have large brains and usually four legs. They breathe air and most live on land.

All mammals give birth to live young, except for the two types that lay eggs. Marsupial mammals have special pouches, where their tiny, partly developed young can continue to grow. Placental mammals give birth to fully formed babies. All mammals make milk in their bodies to feed their offspring. There are about 4,150 species of mammals, divided into 21 groups.

Brown Rat

The largest group of mammals are the rodents. Rats, prairie dogs, squirrels, and mice are all types of rodents.

Koalas are marsupial mammals found only in Australia.

Koala Bear

Ouakari

The ouakari is one of the primates, the most intelligent group of mammals.

Zebra

Zebras belong to the group of hoofed mammals. They walk on the tip of their one "toe," or hoof.

Mammals that live in the sea include seals, dolphins, and whales.

Dolphin

Like most mammals, dolphins give birth to live young.

Where Animals Live

Some kinds of animals can live almost anywhere in the world. But most animals are able to live in only one type of environment. An environment is an area such as a hot desert, a cool grassy plain, or a steamy jungle.

Each environment has its own kind of weather and landscape, and its own plant and animal life. Where the same sorts of environments exist in different parts of the world, similar kinds of animals are found in them.

Poles and Tundra
The North and South Poles, and the Arctic tundra, are very cold places. The winters are long and dark, and the summers very short. These areas, especially the northern ones, are home to a surprising number of animals.

The Cold Forests
South of the tundra, huge forests of coniferous, or cone-bearing, trees stretch right across northern Asia and Europe, Alaska, Canada, and the northern U.S. Here the winters are cold and long, but the summers are warmer than on the tundra. The cold forests provide food and shelter for many different animals.

Deserts
Poles and Tundra
Mountain Ranges
Wetlands
Grasslands
Cold Forests
Tropical Rain Forests
Temperate Woodlands

North America
Brown Bear
Wolf
Raccoon
American Bison
Coyote
White-tailed Deer
Caribou
Moose
Prairie Dog
Skunk
Jackrabbit
Mountain Lion
American Alligator

South America
Giant Armadillo
Sloth
Spider Monkey
Capybara
Vicuña
Jaguar
Anteater
Giant Anaconda
Maned Wolf
Common Iguana
Spectacled Caiman
Howler Monkey

Grasslands
The temperate grasslands are huge grassy plains that stretch for thousands of miles across North and South America, Europe, and Asia. The African grasslands, called savanna, lie near the Equator. Grasslands are home to a huge variety of grazing animals and the predators that hunt them.

Tropical Rain Forests
Dense, steamy jungles are found close to the Equator in the warmest parts of the world. The weather is always hot, and it rains almost every day. The greatest variety of all animal and plant species live in these rain forests.

8

Europe

- Wild Boar
- Red Deer
- Hedgehog
- Rabbit
- Fox
- Adder
- Badger
- Frog
- Red Squirrel
- Lynx
- Otter
- Wild Cat

Temperate Woodlands

Forests and woods of deciduous trees – trees that drop their leaves in the autumn – grow in the milder temperate regions of the world. Here the weather is neither very cold nor hot, and there is plenty of rain.

Mountains

Mountain ranges are found all over the world. Their environments are varied because the climate at the bottom of a mountain is very different from that at the top. Each level has its own plant and animal life.

Wetlands

Swamps, marshes, and other waterlogged regions are found all around the world. Some are freshwater but those on the coasts are saltwater. The dense reeds, grasses, and water plants provide homes and food for the many animals that live partly on land and partly in water.

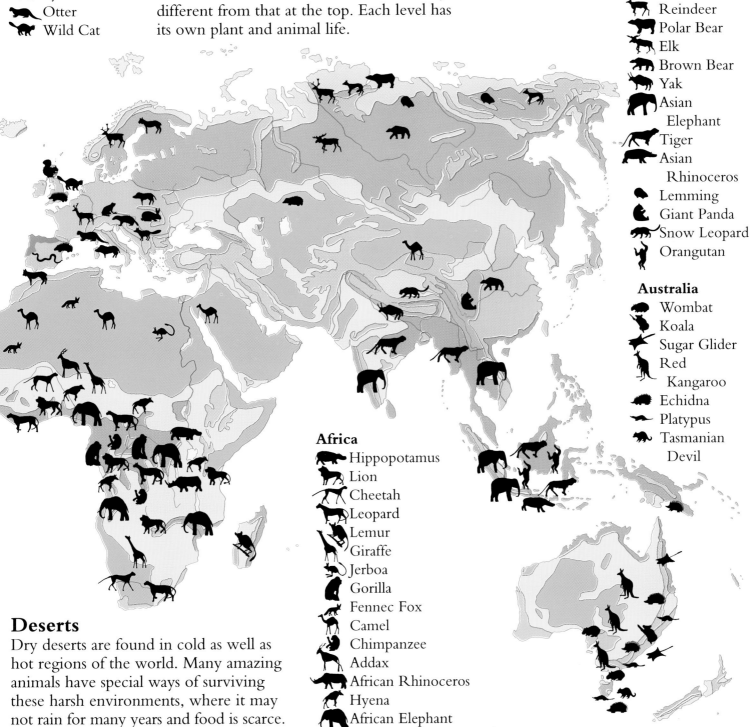

Asia

- Arctic Fox
- Reindeer
- Polar Bear
- Elk
- Brown Bear
- Yak
- Asian Elephant
- Tiger
- Asian Rhinoceros
- Lemming
- Giant Panda
- Snow Leopard
- Orangutan

Australia

- Wombat
- Koala
- Sugar Glider
- Red Kangaroo
- Echidna
- Platypus
- Tasmanian Devil

Africa

- Hippopotamus
- Lion
- Cheetah
- Leopard
- Lemur
- Giraffe
- Jerboa
- Gorilla
- Fennec Fox
- Camel
- Chimpanzee
- Addax
- African Rhinoceros
- Hyena
- African Elephant

Deserts

Dry deserts are found in cold as well as hot regions of the world. Many amazing animals have special ways of surviving these harsh environments, where it may not rain for many years and food is scarce.

In the Desert

Deserts cover about one fifth of the Earth's surface. They are the driest places in the world, with less than 10 in (25 cm) of rain each year. Only a few hardy plants, such as cacti, can grow where there is hardly any water. In this North American desert, the giant saguaro cactus provides a good home, as well as food and moisture, for many desert animals.

Deserts
of the world

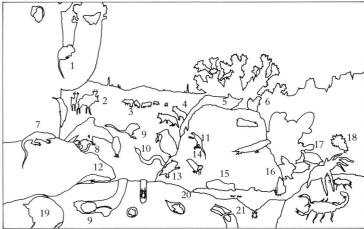

1 Pack Rat	**12** Gila Monster
2 Mule Deer	**13** Horned Lizard
3 Peccary	**14** Grasshopper Mouse
4 Coyote	**15** Diamondback
5 Cacomistle	Rattlesnake
6 Chipmunk	**16** Jack Rabbit
7 Collared Lizard	**17** Desert Tortoise
8 King Snake	**18** Skunk
9 Kangaroo Rat	**19** Kit Fox
10 Sidewinder	**20** Pocket Mouse
11 Spiny Lizard	**21** Bull Snake

In the Scorching Sun

Most deserts, such as the Sahara in Africa, the largest desert in the world, are burning hot during the day and cold at night. A few, such as the Gobi desert in Asia, are bitterly cold in the winter. Some are bare and rocky while others are covered with sand and have huge sand dunes.

Animals that live in the desert have to survive the scorching heat. Many have very little water to drink or even none at all. They shelter under rocks or in holes during the hottest part of the day, coming out at night to hunt for food. Some have special ways of keeping cool, and for living without food and water for long periods.

To protect its eyes from fierce sandstorms, a camel has two rows of eyelashes.

It can also close up its nostrils completely.

Camels do not have much fat under their skin to keep in their body heat.

Useful Humps
Dromedaries, camels with one hump, live in the deserts of Africa and Arabia. Their bodies are perfectly suited to living in such hot, dry places where there is little to eat and drink. After a long time without water, a camel can drink up to 53 gal (200 L) at once.

A Prickly Pair
A coat of spines protects this long-eared hedgehog. It lives in African deserts and eats insects and birds' eggs, feeding on them at night.

When danger threatens, this Indian porcupine can raise its spines and stick them into an enemy.

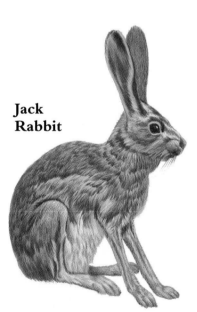

Jack Rabbit

Desert Hedgehog

Indian Porcupine

Big Ears
The North American jack rabbit is really a hare. It has huge ears to help it keep cool and to hear its enemies coming. Babies are covered with fur when they are born.

Desert Jumpers
Large numbers of rodents, such as the desert jerboa, kangaroo mouse, and naked-soled gerbil, live in burrows in the desert. To escape from an enemy, such as a kit fox, they jump high, kicking sand into the fox's face, and then hop away.

Jerboa

Gerbil

Kangaroo Mouse

12

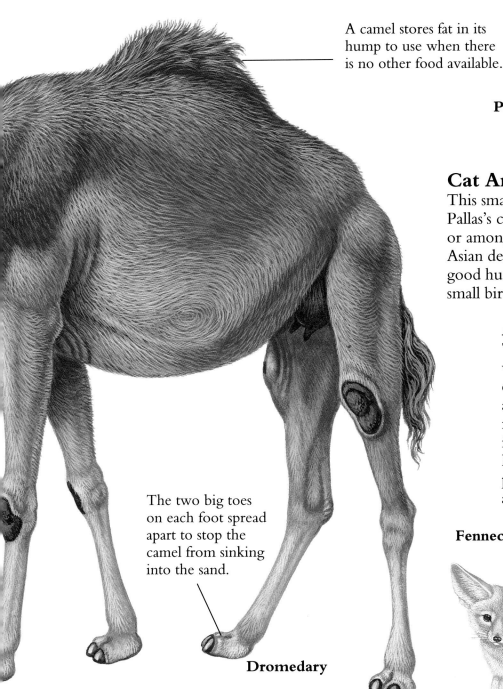

A camel stores fat in its hump to use when there is no other food available.

Pallas's Cat

Cat Among the Rocks

This small wildcat, called Pallas's cat, lives in burrows or among the rocks of Asian deserts. It is a very good hunter and feeds on small birds and rodents.

A Nondrinker

The addax antelope, which lives in the Sahara, does not need to drink any water and gets moisture from the plants it eats. It has very good hearing, which helps to protect it from approaching enemies.

Addax Antelope

Fennec Fox

Kit Fox

The two big toes on each foot spread apart to stop the camel from sinking into the sand.

Dromedary

Desert Facts

The Sahara, the world's largest desert, is nearly as big as the U.S.

Strong winds blowing across the desert pile up the sand into big dunes. Some are over 820 ft (250 m) high and 62 mi (100 km) long.

Many of the animals living in hot deserts never drink water at all.

Temperatures as high as 134°F (56.7°C) have been recorded in the Death Valley, California, and as low as –40°F (–40°C) in the Gobi.

Night Hunters

These two foxes belong to different families. The kit fox lives in the deserts of North America and the fennec fox has its home in Africa.

Both foxes live in holes, coming out at night to catch lizards and birds.

They use their large ears to listen for and track down their prey.

The fennec fox also uses its ears to help keep itself cool. It holds them up so they act as radiators to carry away heat from its furry body.

The Best Survivors

Reptiles are very good at surviving in hot, dry deserts. Unlike birds and mammals, they are cold-blooded and rely on the sun to warm them up. When it gets too hot, some reptiles can change their color or shape to catch as little sun as possible.

Their tough, leathery skins protect them from their enemies and keep in water, so they need little to drink.

Leathery-skinned Lizards

These strange looking creatures live in the deserts of Australia. At night, protected by their tough, scaly skins, they come out of their hiding places to hunt for food. They mostly feed on insects.

Stump-tailed Skink

Blue-tongued Skink

Stump-tailed skinks store fat in their tails to use when there is no food to eat.

To scare away its enemies, this skink opens its mouth, hisses, and sticks out its bright blue tongue.

This legless lizard, which looks more like a snake, feeds mostly on geckos.

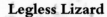

Legless Lizard

Fat-tailed Gecko

Spiny Bush Gecko

The spiny bush gecko wipes foul-smelling liquid over an attacker's face.

The fat-tailed gecko lives in old spider holes and blocks the entrance with its tail.

A Warning Rattle

The poisonous rattlesnake shakes the rattle on the end of its tail as a warning to its enemies.

At night, it hunts for small animals, such as desert rats. Pits in its jaw and its sensitive forked tongue help the snake to detect its prey.

Rattlesnake

When an animal passes the snake's hiding place, it strikes swiftly, sinking its fangs into the victim.

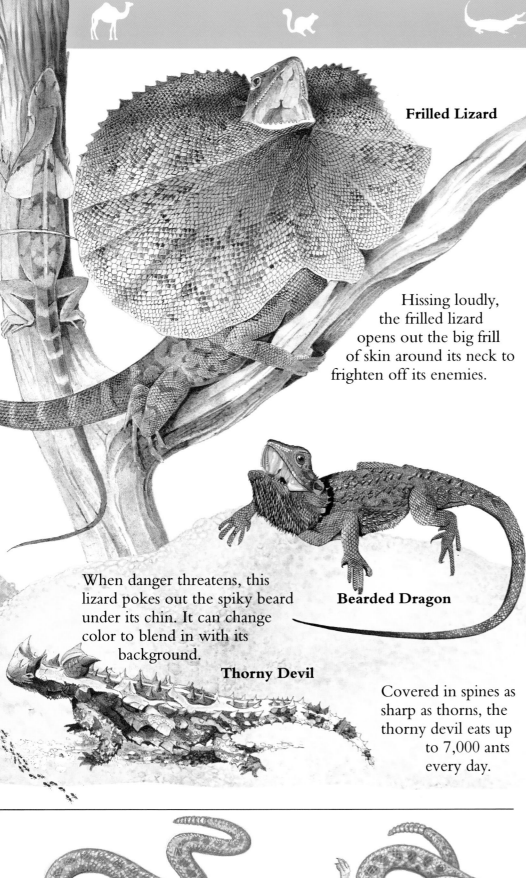

Frilled Lizard

Hissing loudly, the frilled lizard opens out the big frill of skin around its neck to frighten off its enemies.

Bearded Dragon

When danger threatens, this lizard pokes out the spiky beard under its chin. It can change color to blend in with its background.

Thorny Devil

Covered in spines as sharp as thorns, the thorny devil eats up to 7,000 ants every day.

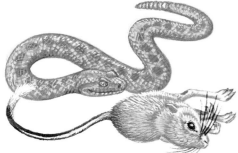

Poison from the snake's fangs goes into the animal's body but does not kill it right away.

Silently, the snake tracks the injured animal until it falls over and dies, and then swallows it whole.

Strange Survivors

Gila Monster

The big gila monster lives in American deserts and is very poisonous. It has a special gland full of poison in its lower jaw.

Desert Tortoise

Under their shells, desert tortoises have special sacs for storing moisture. Their shells protect them from the heat, and the cold.

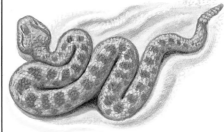

Sidewinder Rattlesnake

Fastest of all North American rattlesnakes, the sidewinder "flows" across the desert, hardly touching the hot sand.

"Sandfish" Skink

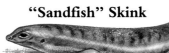

Called the "sandfish," this skink seems to swim through the sand. It moves more like a snake than a lizard.

At the World's Ends

The North and South poles are the coldest places on Earth. There is no land in the Arctic, at the North Pole – only a floating island of ice. The animals there live on the ice and in the cold ocean around it. Very few animals live in the Antarctic, at the South Pole, except in the icy seas. Between the North Pole and the forests of North America, Europe, and Asia is the tundra. This is a wide, flat stretch of bleak land. In winter, the tundra is covered in snow. In summer the top 20 in (50 cm) of ground thaws but the soil beneath stays frozen.

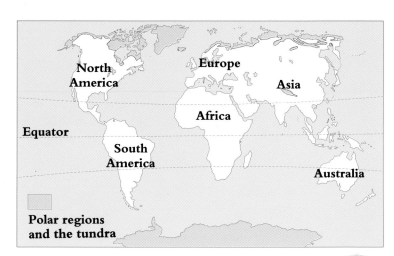

North America
Europe
Asia
Africa
Equator
South America
Australia

Polar regions and the tundra

1 Timber Wolf
2 Polar Bear
3 Tundra Vole
4 Stoat
5 Moose
6 Caribou
7 Wolverine

8 Musk Ox
9 Arctic Fox
10 Arctic Ground Squirrel
11 Wapiti
12 Grizzly Bear
13 Lemming
14 Arctic Hare

A Frozen World

The Arctic winter can last for eight or nine months and the temperature in midsummer never rises above 50°F (10°C). Trees cannot grow here, but a few plants, such as mosses and shrubs, do grow on the flat tundra.

To stay alive in the freezing cold, Arctic animals must be able to stay warm and find enough food. Many Arctic animals are warm-blooded mammals, with thick fur coats that keep in their body heat.

Few animals go into the long, deep sleep called hibernation during the Arctic winter. Instead, they stay active, feeding at the surface or in burrows dug under the snow.

Surviving the Cold

Musk oxen in northern Canada spend the whole winter in the tundra. They travel together in small family herds, searching for food. When threatened by wolves, musk oxen form a circle to protect their calves. Lowered heads and large horns make a good defense.

Musk Ox

Gray Wolf

Arctic Hunters

Polar bears and Arctic foxes are the main hunters, or predators, in the Arctic. Polar bears and grizzly bears sleep through most of the winter, but foxes, wolves, and wolverines hunt throughout the cold months.

Polar Bear

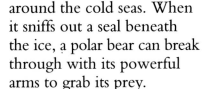

Arctic Fox

Wolf Packs

Gray wolves hunt alone or in packs. They feed mainly on small mammals but will attack musk oxen and caribou, preying on weak animals.

Color Change

An Arctic fox eats small animals and the remains of meals left by polar bears. In winter, its coat turns from gray or brown to white.

Grizzly Bear

Seal Snatcher

Polar bears live on the Arctic coast and hunt in and around the cold seas. When it sniffs out a seal beneath the ice, a polar bear can break through with its powerful arms to grab its prey.

Largest Meat-eaters

Often claimed as the largest living carnivores, grizzly bears also like to eat fruit, honey, and insects as well as small mammals.

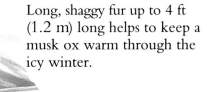

Long, shaggy fur up to 4 ft (1.2 m) long helps to keep a musk ox warm through the icy winter.

A thick layer of fat, built up during the short summer, also protects it against the cold.

Poles and Tundra Facts

The lowest temperature on Earth, -128.6°F (-89.2°C) was recorded in the Antarctic in 1983.

The Poles are cold because they are the two places on Earth that are farthest away from the sun.

The word "tundra" is Finnish and means "treeless plain."

In the Arctic, the sun never sets in summer and it is daylight all the time. In winter, the sun never rises and the days are cold and dark.

Burrowers

Mice, lemmings, and voles survive the harsh Arctic winter in burrows beneath the snow. These small rodents live on their stores of hay and seeds from last year's crop.

Arctic Ground Squirrel

Large Population

Lemmings, like this Arctic lemming, are able to produce many babies and their numbers can build up fast. In some years, there are so many of them in one area that food is scarce. Huge numbers then swarm away to find new homes.

Warm Bed

An Arctic ground squirrel is unusual because it hibernates inside a warm burrow for the whole winter. It spends the summer fattening up, ready for its next long winter sleep.

Arctic Lemming

Deer Hunter

Although a wolverine is rather slow and clumsy, it sometimes traps prey as large as deer, using its cunning and patience. It usually feeds on small mammals and berries.

Stoat

Ruthless Killers

Expert runners and climbers, ferocious stoats will hunt and kill any animal up to the size of a hare. Stoats, in their turn, are trapped by hunters when they turn white for the Arctic winter. Their beautiful coats are then known as ermine, a much-prized fur.

Wolverine

Arctic Hare

Winter Disguise

The white winter coat of an Arctic hare makes it hard to see against the snow. This helps to protect the hare from predators when it comes out of its burrow to search for food.

19

Land of the Deer

The Arctic spring comes in April or May, and on the tundra, the snow quickly disappears. During the summer months, the tundra is a rich feeding ground for many mammals, birds, and insects. The largest plant-eaters, or herbivores, are the caribou, called reindeer in Europe. They move from the forests in the south, where they have spent the winter, to feed on the new grass and lichens and to spend the summer in the tundra.

A Dangerous Journey

When the summer ends, the caribou, or reindeer, begin the long journey south to the pine forests. The herd may travel long distances and face many dangers on the way. They may be stopped by early blizzards, and they may have to swim icy rivers. Wolves and other predators are always lurking nearby.

In the shelter and safety of the pine forests, the caribou scrape away the snow to find lichen and moss to eat. The caribou cows are now carrying unborn calves. They will give birth to the calves when they return to the tundra the following summer.

Close Relations

These deer live in North America and in northern Europe and Asia. Some are the same species but have different names in different parts of the world. Only caribou, or reindeer, are true tundra dwellers.

Forest Giant

Moose live in the northern forests of North America. The largest of the deer, a male moose may stand nearly 6 ft (2 m) high.

Females with Antlers

The female caribou of North America grow antlers as well as the males. This is unusual among deer.

Smaller Cousins

Red deer live in Europe and parts of Asia.

Wapiti

Wapiti are the second largest deer. They live mostly in the Rocky Mountain region of the United States.

Moose

Caribou

Red Deer

Wapiti

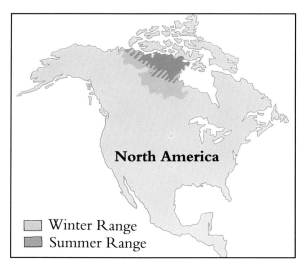

Regular Routes

Barren-ground caribou may travel distances of up to 500 mi (800 km). They move to and from the tundra along the same paths each year. In some places, 2 ft (60 cm) of rock has been worn away by the thousands of deer that have passed through on migration.

Growth of Deer Antlers

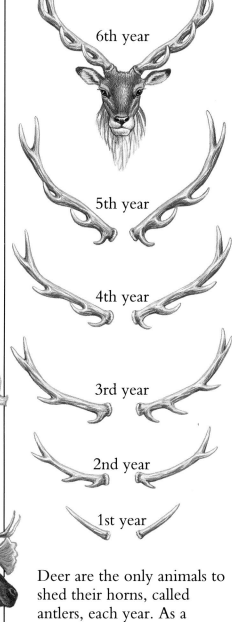

6th year

5th year

4th year

3rd year

2nd year

1st year

Winter Range
Summer Range

North America

Huge Horns

North American moose are the same as European elk. Their enormous horns may measure up to 4 ft (1.2 m) across. The chief hunters of these animals are wolves. They usually use their hooves, rather than their horns, to defend themselves against predators.

Domestic Herds

Reindeer of Europe and Asia are the same as caribou of North America. They are now all domesticated – tamed by people – and looked after by wandering herders.

European Elk

Reindeer

Deer are the only animals to shed their horns, called antlers, each year. As a deer grows older, its new antlers get bigger and begin to grow prongs. At first, new antlers have a soft, skinlike covering called "velvet." The velvet peels off, or is rubbed off, when the antlers are fully grown and have become hard.

Up in the Clouds

The mountains of the world cover about one twentieth of the land surface. In the tallest range, the Himalayas, is Mount Everest, the highest point on Earth. The tops of high mountains are very cold, often covered with snow all year-round, and with strong winds blowing. The air is thin, and some people who climb the mountains need extra oxygen to breathe. The animals that live there have thick fur to keep them warm.

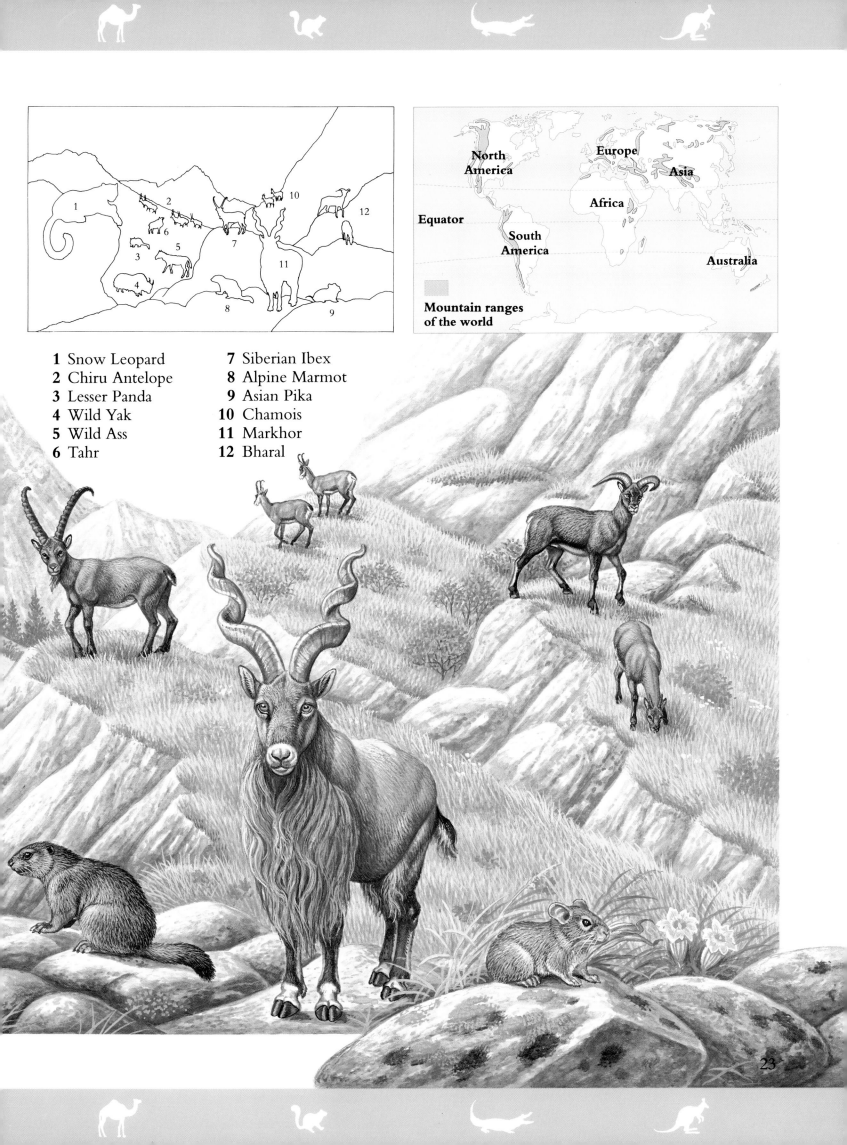

North America
Europe
Asia
Equator
Africa
South America
Australia

Mountain ranges of the world

1 Snow Leopard
2 Chiru Antelope
3 Lesser Panda
4 Wild Yak
5 Wild Ass
6 Tahr
7 Siberian Ibex
8 Alpine Marmot
9 Asian Pika
10 Chamois
11 Markhor
12 Bharal

The High Life

A wide variety of animals live on mountains, because the weather lower down is so different from the weather higher up. Tropical forests grow on the foothills of Mount Kilimanjaro, in Africa, and there is snow and ice all year-round on the top.

To survive, mountain animals must be adapted to their surroundings. Sheep and goats are surefooted climbers. Reptiles and amphibians are usually dark so that their bodies absorb the sun's warmth. Mammals that live in the colder places have thick fur and short, round ears to keep them from losing body heat.

An enlarged heart helps the bear to cope with the thin mountain air.

White "spectacle" markings on the bear's face differ in shape from one animal to another.

Andean Spectacled Bear

Bear with "Glasses"

Andean spectacled bears live high in the paramo, or grassy plains, 11,800 ft (3,600 m) up in the Andes mountains. They are the only South American bears and get their name from their markings.

Strong claws help it climb up tall trees to reach the leaves to eat.

Big Eaters

The big mountain cats prey on the large grazing animals. Mountain lions hunt in the forests of the Rockies, in North America. Also called cougars, they attack animals as big as deer.

Mountain Lion

Himalayan Cat

The beautiful snow leopard lives in the Himalayas, mostly above the snow line. Its main prey is the Siberian ibex, a big-horned goat.

Snow Leopard

24

Mountain Climbers

Many kinds of hoofed animals graze on the high slopes of the Himalayas. Large herds of chiru antelope, as well as small groups of yaks, roam the highest slopes, sometimes wandering up to about 20,000 ft (6,100 m). Wild asses, Tibetan gazelles, and the various kinds of wild sheep prefer the lower slopes. In winter, most of these animals move down the mountains to find food.

Chiru Antelope

Yak

Bharal

Tibetan Gazelle

Tibetan Wild Ass

Nayan

Shapu

Swimming Mole

The strange Pyrenean desman lives in the Pyrenees. A long-nosed, swimming mole, it eats water creatures from mountain streams.

Pyrenean Desman

Cave Dweller

Mountain salamanders live on the Alps and Pyrenees mountains of Europe. They are amphibians and are related to newts but spend most of their time on land. They sometimes live in caves.

Alpine Salamander

Mountain Toad

This toad lives in the high Andes. It hunts by day, hiding away at night.

Mountain Toad

Himalayan Pit Viper

Top Snake

Himalayan pit vipers live higher up than any other snake.

Largest Mountain Mammal

Yaks are the largest of the mountain mammals. Huge males may be over 6 ft (2 m) tall at the shoulder. Yaks can survive at heights of 20,000 ft (6,100 m), protected from the cold by their thick, matted coats. Up on the high, bleak slopes, they often feed only on mosses and lichens.

Mountain Facts

The highest mountains in the world are the Rockies, Andes, Alps, Pyrenees, and Himalayas.

The higher you go up a mountain, the colder it gets. The temperature drops by 3.6°F (2°C) every 990 ft (300 m).

The youngest mountain ranges were pushed up about 60 to 70 million years ago.

Fossils of sea shells found high up on some mountains prove that they were once at the bottom of the sea.

Yak

A Watery World

There are rivers, streams, lakes, and ponds all over the world. Many different animals live in or around them. At the coast, where fresh water meets the sea, the wildlife changes again. Wetlands are waterlogged nearly all the time. They include swamps, marshes, bogs, and fens and can be freshwater or salty. Some wetlands are covered with tough grasses, others with trees. They all have a lot of plant life and are home to an amazing variety of animals.

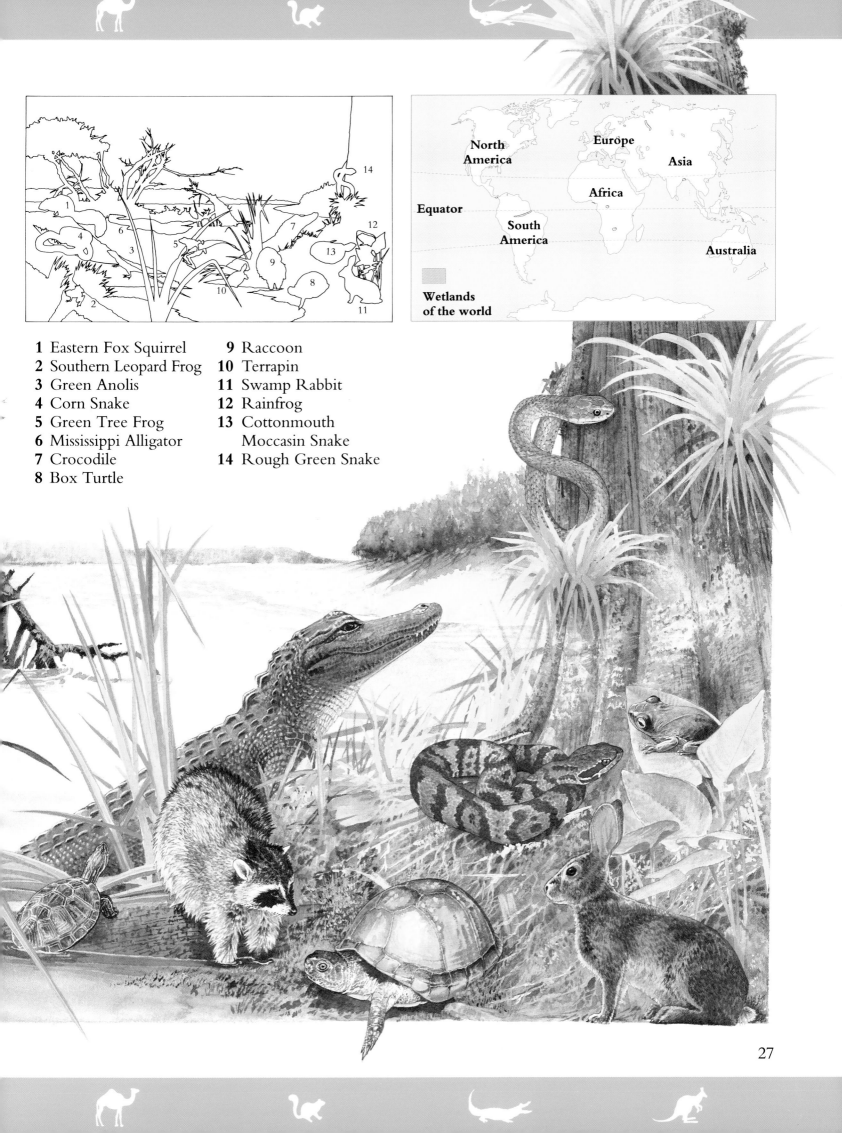

1 Eastern Fox Squirrel
2 Southern Leopard Frog
3 Green Anolis
4 Corn Snake
5 Green Tree Frog
6 Mississippi Alligator
7 Crocodile
8 Box Turtle
9 Raccoon
10 Terrapin
11 Swamp Rabbit
12 Rainfrog
13 Cottonmouth
   Moccasin Snake
14 Rough Green Snake

North America
Europe
Asia
Africa
Equator
South America
Australia

Wetlands of the world

Marsh Creatures

In the wetlands, the plants grow so close together that the water often flows very slowly and lacks oxygen. Reptiles that live in water, such as crocodiles and turtles, can survive because they breathe air.

Tropical swamps and marshes are home to many kinds of snakes. They glide among the plants and swim in the water, hunting reptiles, birds, frogs, and small mammals. Voles and otters, with waterproof fur and webbed feet, are perfectly suited to their watery world.

A Graceful Heavyweight

Water-loving hippopotamuses are the biggest animals in the African wetlands. They can measure 16 ft (4.9 m) long and weigh 3.5 tons. Clumsy on land, hippos are graceful swimmers and divers. They can even give birth and nurse their babies in water.

They live in groups and spend their days wallowing in swamps and rivers, feeding on water cabbage. At night, hippos leave the water to graze on dry land.

Underwater Cover

The shy sitatunga antelope grazes on water plants. Its long, banana-shaped hooves spread out to stop it from sinking into soft mud. If danger threatens, a sitatunga plunges into the water. It hides there, with only its nostrils showing so that it can breathe.

Hippos produce slimy pink "sweat" that helps to keep their skin healthy.

Hippo tusks may be over 3 ft (1 m) long.

A hippo's gaping yawn is a challenge to fight another hippo.

Hippopotamus   **Sitatunga**

Capybara

Largest Rodent
Amazon capybaras are the largest rodents. They are about as big as sheep. At dawn and dusk, large groups feed on water plants.

Muskrat

Herald Snake

Winter Hide-out
Muskrats are the largest North American voles. They live in lakes and rivers, hiding among the water plants in summer. In winter, they build houses of plants above the water line.

Spectacled Caiman

Hunted Hunter
Spectacled caimans live in the waters of the Amazon River. Related to crocodiles and alligators, they eat capybaras and are hunted for their skins. They swim swiftly through the water, lashing their powerful tails.

Cannibal
This American alligator lives in the Florida Everglades and grows up to 12 ft (3.5 m) long. When food is scarce, it hunts otters and may sometimes eat small alligators.

American Alligator

Swamp and Marsh Facts

African swamps are natural reservoirs. During the rainy season they collect and store water, releasing it in the dry season.

European freshwater marshes are full of bird life. Foxes, stoats, and – in Spain – lynxes hunt for food in the dry parts.

In the dry season, some Everglades alligators dig water holes. They break the hard ground with their tails and use their snouts as shovels.

Crocodiles float just underwater with only eyes and nostrils showing. They swallow stones to keep balanced in the water.

Mother Love
Nile crocodiles have powerful jaws and can kill and eat an animal as big as a cow. The females are caring mothers and gently carry their young from place to place between their very sharp teeth.

Nile Crocodile

A Tropical Swamp

In the hot tropical regions of the world, forests of mangrove trees grow in the mud of many coastal swamps. The high, tangled roots of the trees and other swamp plants trap mud and waste matter carried down by rivers. They also trap matter that is washed in by the sea.

This rich mud provides homes and food for the swamp animals, which spend half of their lives on land and half in salt water.

Proboscis Monkey

Dusky Langur

Silvered Langur

Big-nosed Monkey

The male proboscis monkey has a huge nose that hangs down over its mouth. He has to push it out of the way to eat. When he makes warning sounds, his nose helps to amplify the booming noises he makes. The female monkeys have short, upturned noses.

Daytime Moonrat

A moonrat uses its long, sensitive nose to sniff out insects, earthworms, and snails. It hunts in the day and hides at night in holes under trees.

Very few monkeys live in mangrove forests.

All these monkeys live on fruit and the leaves of swamp plants.

Malayan Moonrat

Bright Orange Babies

The babies of silvered langurs are bright orange and have black hands when they are born. They change to the adult color when they are about three months old. Each mother looks after her baby until it is about 15 months old.

Leaf Lover

A dusky langur eats up to 4 lb (2 kg) of leaves and plants a day. It lives in groups of 3 to 20 animals that move about in the trees to feed. Langurs are peaceful creatures that seldom fight each other.

Seafood Specialists

Crab-eating macaques feed on fruit, insects, and amphibians. They also fish in shallow water, picking up crabs and shellfish.

These monkeys live in groups of up to 30, led by two or more males. They have a strict social order and band together to fight when threatened by a predator. Macaques spend most of their time on the ground but will climb trees to find shelter or to look for food.

Crab-eating Macaque

Mangrove Reptiles

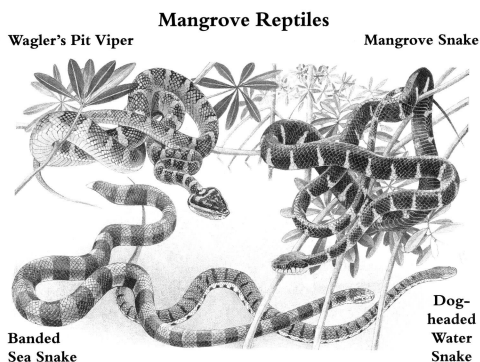

Wagler's Pit Viper

Mangrove Snake

Banded Sea Snake

Dog-headed Water Snake

Sinister Snakes

Mangrove snakes wrap themselves around plants and trees and search for birds and their eggs.

Dog-headed water snakes and banded sea snakes hunt for fish and crabs. Pit vipers have a heat-sensitive pit between their eyes and nostrils. This detects changes in temperature when warm-blooded prey is nearby.

Fierce Predator

Monitor lizards are fierce animals with sharp teeth and claws. They eat snakes, birds, and smaller animals as well as fish and shellfish. They can open their jaws in such a way that they can swallow very large prey. Monitors live in many different habitats, including mangrove swamps.

Monitor Lizard

Crab-eating Frog

Crab-hunter

This large frog hunts for crabs in the swamps and for insects on land.

The Rolling Grasslands

Huge grassy plains stretch over vast regions of the Earth. They grow between the areas where there is not enough rain for trees and the dry semideserts. They are known by different names in different parts of the world. In North America they are called the prairies, and in South America, the pampas. In northern Europe and Asia, they are known as the steppes, and in Africa, the savanna.

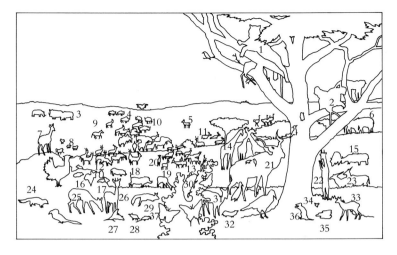

1 Leopard	**6** Elephant	**13** Impala	**20** Thomson's
2 Vervet Monkey	**7** Klipspringer	**14** Kenyan Giraffe	Gazelle
3 White	**8** Anubis Baboon	**15** African Buffalo	**21** Greater Koodoo
Rhinoceros	**9** Burchell's Zebra	**16** Bat-eared Fox	**22** Gerenuk
4 Wildebeest	**10** Topi	**17** Rock Hyrax	**23** Eland
5 Common	**11** Red Lechwe	**18** Warthog	**24** Zoril
Waterbuck	**12** Kob	**19** Steenbok	

25 Oribi	
26 Austrida	
27 Field Mouse	
28 Elephant Shrew	
29 Spring Hare	
30 Chameleon	

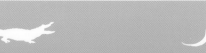

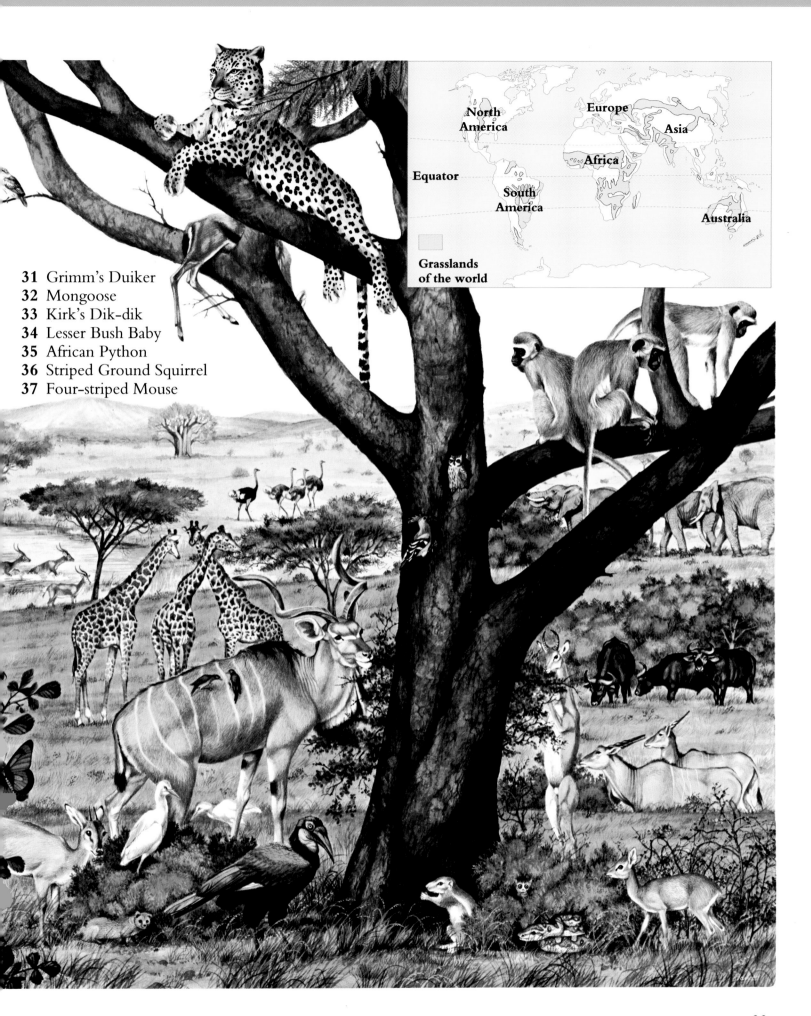

31 Grimm's Duiker
32 Mongoose
33 Kirk's Dik-dik
34 Lesser Bush Baby
35 African Python
36 Striped Ground Squirrel
37 Four-striped Mouse

North
America

Europe

Asia

Equator

Africa

South
America

Australia

Grasslands
of the world

Grassland Animals

Huge herds of large grazing animals once roamed the vast grasslands of the world. Many of the animals were hunted almost to extinction and parts of their grazing lands taken over for farming. The predators that followed the herds also declined as there was less food for them. Today, the herds of some of the animals have built up again, and many are protected from hunting by law.

Many kinds of small grassland animals spend all their lives in one place. They dig out their burrows, sometimes with thousands of animals sharing a great network of underground tunnels. They eat roots, leaves, and seeds, coming out from their burrows to feed at night.

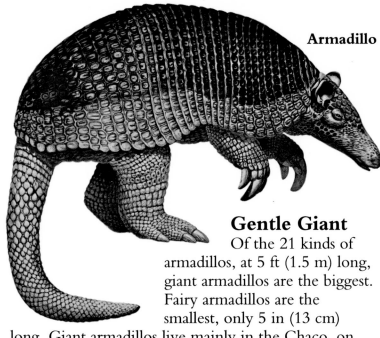

Armadillo

Gentle Giant

Of the 21 kinds of armadillos, at 5 ft (1.5 m) long, giant armadillos are the biggest. Fairy armadillos are the smallest, only 5 in (13 cm) long. Giant armadillos live mainly in the Chaco, on the edge of the South American pampas. They like to live close to water and are most active at night. Although they can weigh 110 lb (50 kg), they move quickly and gracefully.

Treetops to Lowest Leaves

Savanna plant-eaters often feed in the same place, but because the animals are at different heights, they eat different parts of the plants and trees. Monkeys in the treetops reach the highest leaves. Giraffes can stretch up to feed 20 ft (6 m) above the ground. Next come the elephants with their long trunks. Gerenuk antelopes can balance on their hind legs to reach the lower branches. Other types of antelopes, such as elands and koodoos, and black rhinoceroses also feed at this level, as well as grazing on grass. Tiny dik-diks eat the lowest leaves, while warthogs sniff out roots and bulbs on the ground.

1 Springbok
2 Eland
3 Koodoo
4 Giraffe
5 Warthog
6 Black Rhinoceros
7 Elephant
8 Vervet Monkey
9 Gerenuk
10 Steenbok
11 Kirk's Dik-dik

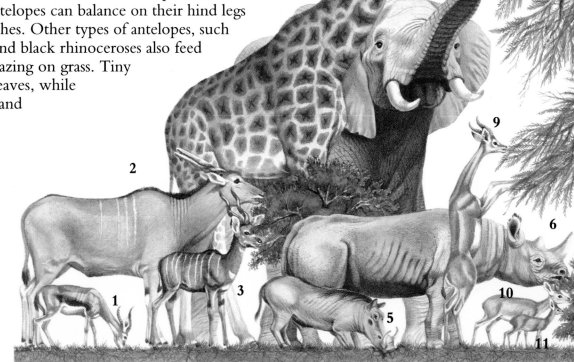

Marbled Polecat

Prairie Killer

The marbled polecat hunts the small prairie burrowers. It even shares the underground homes of the animals it eats.

European Suslik

Prairie Dog

Burrowing Squirrel

Prairie dogs are really burrowing squirrels. These North American rodents are preyed upon by animals such as badgers, coyotes, and large birds.

Skilled Engineers

European susliks live together in complicated underground tunnel systems with thousands of exits and entrances.

South American Camel

Guanacos are a kind of llama, a smaller relative of the camel. Guanacos live in small herds of one male and a few females with their young. They wander the dry southern grasslands of South America, grazing on prairie grass and tough bushes.

Precious Horns

Large-nosed saiga antelopes live on the barren Asian steppes. They were once hunted especially for their horns. The horns were ground into powder and used in Chinese medicine.

Saiga Antelope

Guanaco Llama

Deadly Squeeze

Snakes of the North American prairies feed on the many rodents. Bull snakes are not poisonous. They kill by coiling around their prey, squeezing it to death.

American Bison

Bull Snake

A Ton Weight

Also known as buffalo, American bison are huge. Large males can weigh over a ton. Their long, shaggy winter coats fall off in patches in the spring, making them look untidy.

The Hunters

The animals that rule the grasslands are those that hunt other animals. They are the predators and include the big cats and the hunting dogs. They prey on animals both large and small. Once the hunters have eaten their fill after a kill, the grassland scavengers move in to finish what is left. The African savanna, with its huge range of animal life, is home to more predators than any other grassland region.

Pride of the Savanna

Very few cats live in large groups but lions are unusual. They live in groups, called prides, of about 15 animals, headed by a leading male. Large males may reach 10 ft (3 m) in length and measure 3 ft (1 m) tall at the shoulder. A lion's magnificent mane grows on its head, shoulders, and neck, and sometimes on its stomach. Its loud roar can often be heard in the early morning, but it always hunts silently.

Lion's Share

Lionesses, working in teams, do most of the hunting. They follow the herds of zebras, gazelles, and wildebeest, and will even attack giraffes. They usually single out a weak or lone animal from a herd and stalk it slowly before springing to the attack. After a kill, the males feed first, followed by the females and then the cubs. Lions never kill more than the pride needs to eat.

Lioness

Lion

Black Leopard

Leopards with almost all-black coats are known as black panthers. Their hidden spots can be seen in bright sunlight.

Black Panther

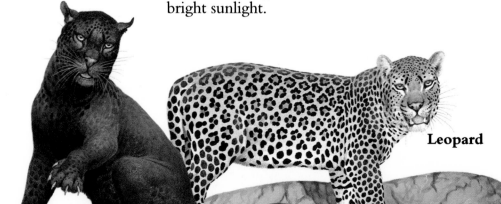

Leopard

Surprise Attack

Leopards eat birds, monkeys, and other small grassland animals as well as larger herbivores such as wildebeest. They hunt alone, stalking their prey until they are close enough to pounce. Older leopards will sometimes lie in wait on a tree branch, dropping down suddenly on top of their victims.

Hyena

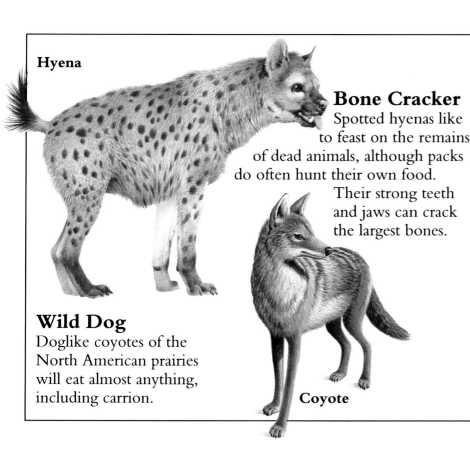

Bone Cracker
Spotted hyenas like to feast on the remains of dead animals, although packs do often hunt their own food. Their strong teeth and jaws can crack the largest bones.

Scavengers of the Plains
Scavengers feed on carrion, which is meat from dead animals.

Jackal

Wild Dog
Doglike coyotes of the North American prairies will eat almost anything, including carrion.

Coyote

Grassland Cleaners
Jackals, usually smaller than hyenas, are also scavengers. By eating carrion, these animals play an important part in keeping the grasslands clean.

Speed Champion
Cheetahs are the fastest land animals. Over about 440 yd (400 m), they can reach over 60 mph (100 kph). A cheetah's long legs and flexible spine help it to move quickly. It grows up to 1 ft (30 cm) taller than a leopard of the same length. Cheetahs prey on animals such as gazelles by first stalking and then outrunning them. They kill by gripping their victims by the throat. Once they have eaten, cheetahs usually leave the rest of the kill to scavengers.

Maned Wolf

Nighttime Hunter
Maned wolves are really giant foxes. They live and hunt on the South American plains. Their unusual "manes" run from the base of their necks right down their backs. Maned wolves usually hunt alone, at night.

Cheetah

Killer Pack
African hunting dogs will chase their prey until it is exhausted. A pack of as many as 20 hunts animals as large as zebra. When close enough, they leap onto their prey.

Hunting Dog

The Cold Forests

Huge forests spread almost right across northern Europe and Asia, south of the icy tundra. They make up a region called the taiga. In Canada, Alaska, and parts of the northern United States, the ribbon of forests stretches up to 500 mi (800 km) wide. There it is called the boreal forest.

Cone-bearing trees such as pine and fir grow close together in these cold northern forests. They are often deep in snow for several months each winter.

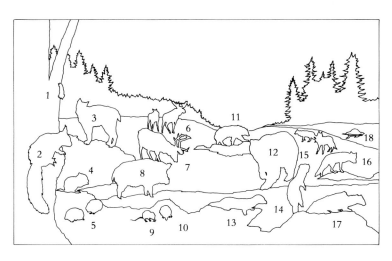

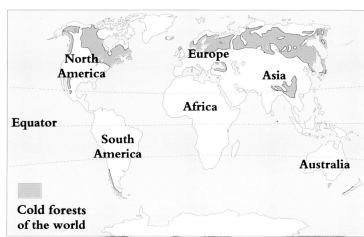

Cold forests
of the world

1 Northern Bat
2 Red Squirrel
3 Lynx
4 Siberian Chipmunk
5 Root Vole
6 Elk/Moose
7 European Reindeer
8 Wild Boar
9 Pygmy Shrew
10 Common Shrew
11 Wolverine
12 Brown Bear
13 Siberian Weasel
14 Stoat
15 Wolf
16 Arctic Fox
17 Pine Marten
18 Beaver

Forest Animals

The northern forests grow on mostly flat land. There are many lakes, slow-flowing streams, and areas of swampy ground. The weather is cold and wet, with long, snowy winters. During the cold months, animals such as badgers and bears hibernate. The many forest rodents survive by feeding on the stores of seeds and nuts they gathered in the summer. They are hunted by predators such as lynx and pine martens.

Another kind of cold forest grows in a highland region of Sichuan, in western China. This is a bamboo forest, home to some unusual animals not found anywhere else.

A giant panda may eat 26 to 30 lb (12 to 14 kg) of bamboo in 24 hours.

"Thumbs" on its front paws help the panda to hold its food.

Strong jaws and teeth are needed for chewing the tough bamboo.

Giant Panda

Brown Bear

Winter Sleep
Brown bears build up thick layers of fat in the autumn. This keeps them alive while they sleep through most of the cold winter months.

Panda Puzzle
Giant pandas live in the cold bamboo forests of the Chinese highlands. They eat mainly bamboo shoots but will also feed on small mammals, birds, and fish. Giant pandas give birth to one or two cubs, but usually only one survives to become an adult. These shy animals are not often seen in the wild.

Under Protection
Enormous European bison, also called wisent, can weigh up to a ton. In the past, these bison were overhunted for their meat. Today, they live in small, protected herds in parts of Poland and the USSR.

European Bison

Wild Boar

Forest Pig
Wild boars find their food on the forest floor, sniffing out roots, insects, and small animals with their piglike snouts. They are strong, fierce creatures, with thick bristly skin and sharp tusks.

Winter Stores

Many rodents live in the northern forests and feed on seeds and nuts. Flying squirrels eat birds' eggs as well as pinecones and berries. Red squirrels keep a winter larder of mushrooms speared on the points of branches.

Eurasian Flying Squirrel

Red Squirrel

Chipmunk

Prey for Eagles

Chipmunks gather a store of seeds and nuts to last the winter. They are preyed upon by owls and eagles.

Skunk

Sable

American Mink

Smelly Skunk

The North American striped skunk hunts small animals along the forest edge. It is famous for the foul smell it makes if it is disturbed or attacked. The smell comes from a liquid that it sprays from glands under its large bushy tail. Some skunks can squirt this fluid as far as 13 ft (4 m), and the odor is so bad that they are left alone by most predators.

Prized Predators

These small, fierce meat-eaters belong to the same family as weasels. They hunt birds, squirrels, voles, and insects. American mink and European and Asian sables were prized for their valuable fur. Sables were especially overhunted but are now protected by law.

Nest Robber

Pine martens of northern Europe have a very varied diet. Expert climbers, they will search through trees to pounce on birds or to rob their nests of eggs. They will also dig up bees' nests to get at the grubs and honey.

Pine Marten

Dam Builders

With their strong teeth, American beavers cut down trees and use them to dam rivers and streams. In the pond formed by the dam, they build a large "lodge" of branches and mud. Each lodge has several "rooms" above the water, where the beavers have their babies.

Beaver

Cold Forest Facts

The Siberian taiga covers an area more than one third bigger than the whole United States.

In certain areas, the bamboo forests are being cut down, threatening the home and food supply of giant pandas. The Chinese government has set up nature reserves for the pandas' protection.

When supplies of food are scarce, moose may strip and eat the bark off of trees. This may cause the trees to die.

The Living Rain Forests

Great, dense forests of huge trees, called tropical rain forests, are found close to the Equator. They are known as tropical rain forests because they grow in areas that have no seasons, and where it is hot and rainy all year.

Rain forest trees grow very close together. Many of them are over 100 ft (30 m) tall, and often have creepers wrapped around their trunks. More kinds of animals live in rain forests than in any other habitat.

North America

Europe

Asia

Africa

Equator

South America

Australia

Rain forests of the world

1 Spider Monkey	**13** Two-toed Sloth
2 Boa Constrictor	**14** Margay
3 Red Howler Monkey	**15** Squirrel Monkey
4 Black Spider Monkey	**16** Geoffrey's Marmoset
5 Tree Porcupine	**17** Four-eyed Opossum
6 Monk Saki	**18** Pygmy Anteater
7 Coatimundi	**19** White-eared Tufted
8 Kinkajou	Marmoset
9 Emerald Tree Boa	**20** Tree Frog
10 Tamarin	**21** Forest Bat
11 Common Iguana	**22** Mouse Opossum
12 Capuchin	**23** Vampire Bat

False Vampire Bat

Rain Forest Creatures

All rain forests have several layers of trees and plants. The top layer may be as high as 80 to 100 ft (25 to 30 m) above the ground. Smaller trees and bushes make a second, lower layer and below this is a third, thick layer of ferns and jungle plants.

The rain forest animals all live at different levels, each with its own feeding ground. Many are good climbers. There are only a few large ground animals. These include elephants in the African jungle and tigers in the rain forests of Southeast Asia.

False Vampire

False vampire bats do not suck blood like true vampire bats. Instead, they hunt small rodents, birds, and insects. They live in Africa and Asia and may have a wingspan of 1 ft (30 cm).

Royal Antelope

Jaguar

Water-loving Cat

South American jaguars like to live close to water. When hunting, they will chase tapirs and capybaras right into the river. Jaguars also catch fish in the river shallows.

Goliath Frog

The tiger's markings help it blend into the forest background.

Biggest and Smallest

Royal antelopes of the African rain forest are the smallest in the world. They are only 1 ft (30 cm) tall. Huge goliath frogs live in the same jungle. Their bodies may grow to a length of 1 ft (30 cm).

Tiger

Like all cats, tigers see well in the dark.

The tiger's sharp teeth can stab and slice at its prey.

Biggest Cat

Tigers are the largest of the big cats. Males may grow up to 10 ft (3 m) long. They are one of the few animals that will kill and eat people. Tigers prey mainly on medium to large mammals, which they hunt during the night.

Powerful claws make dangerous weapons.

44

Chameleon

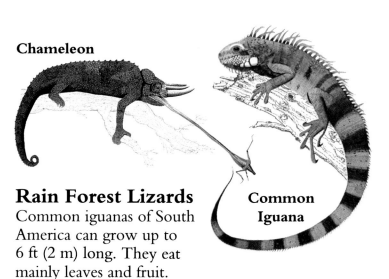

Common Iguana

Rain Forest Lizards

Common iguanas of South America can grow up to 6 ft (2 m) long. They eat mainly leaves and fruit. Chameleons can make each eye look in a different direction at the same time. They can also change skin color to match their background.

Hanging Around

The tree boa of South America hangs down from tree branches and waits for its prey. When a small animal comes near, the boa drops down, wraps itself around its victim, and squeezes it to death.

Tree Boa

Giant Snake

Giant anacondas live in the Amazon rain forests. They grow as long as 30 ft (9 m) and may weigh up to 400 lb (180 kg). Anacondas live near water, where they can prey on the animals that come to drink.

Anaconda

Airborne Animals

These small animals live in the rain forests of Southeast Asia. They are able to escape danger and move from the trees to the ground by gliding. Flying snakes "fly" by flattening their bodies in the air. Gliding frogs use their webbed feet to glide more than 40 to 50 ft (12 to 15 m) between trees.

Flying Snake

Gliding Frog

Winged Mammal

Colugos of the Southeast Asian rain forests can glide from tree to tree on "wings" of loose skin. They are nighttime hunters – by day, they sleep hanging upside down from tree branches, or resting in tree holes.

Colugo

No Teeth

The toothless anteater walks on the backs of its "fingers." These are powerful claws for tearing open termites' nests. The anteater collects thousands of termites with its long sticky tongue.

Hoffman's Sloth

Rain Forest Facts

There are over a million different kinds of plants and animals in the Amazon rain forests. Parts of the forests are being cleared for roads and farms. The destruction of their habitat is putting the animals and plants at risk.

Green Coat

Two-toed South American sloths rest for up to 18 hours a day. They hang upside down from the branch of a tree, even when eating fruit and leaves. Algae growing on their fur give it a greenish color, which makes a good camouflage.

Anteater

Tree Acrobats

Primates are the most intelligent group of mammals, with large, well-developed brains. They include lemurs, monkeys, apes, chimpanzees, and human beings. Many kinds of primates live in the tropical rain forests. The smaller ones usually live high up in the trees, while the larger ones spend most of their time near or on the ground. All primates have five fingers on each hand and five toes on each foot. Some have tails and many can walk almost upright.

Orangutans' arms are one and a half times longer than their legs.

Orangutan

Orangutans can grab onto tree branches with their toes.

Man of the Woods

Orangutan means "man of the woods" in the Malay language. These apes live in the rain forests of Southeast Asia, in pairs or small groups. Among the apes, they are second in intelligence only to chimpanzees. Young orangutans move through the forest swinging by their arms from branch to branch. Older animals move more slowly, walking along branches on all fours.

The hair on an orangutan's shoulders and arms may grow up to 18 in (45 cm) long.

The Greatest Ape

Gorillas are the largest of the great apes. The males are 6 ft (2 m) tall and can weigh 440 lb (200 kg). They live in the African rain forests in family groups of about 15, led by the strongest male. They are vegetarian, eating only plants and fruit. The gorilla looks frightening, but is in fact a very gentle animal. The male hoots and beats his chest if danger threatens but hardly ever attacks.

Chimpanzee

Most Intelligent

Chimpanzees are the most intelligent primates, apart from human beings. They live in family groups in the African rain forest, and feed on fruit and plants as well as insects, eggs, and young birds. Chimps are noisy and excitable, and will greet other chimps by touching and kissing.

Gorilla

Diana
Monkey

Colobus
Monkey

Moustache Monkey

Life in the Trees

All of these African monkeys spend a lot of time moving through the trees, looking for fruit, insects, and plants to eat. They are all lightweight, so that they can reach leaves and fruit at the ends of even the thinnest branches. These monkeys are sometimes preyed on by eagles, which swoop down from above. Lower down, they must watch out for pythons and leopards.

Spider
Monkey

A Gripping Tail

A spider monkey's long limbs and tail help it to move gracefully through the South American rain forest. Its tail is specially adapted for gripping onto tree branches. Spider monkeys can even use their tails to pick up small objects, such as seeds and nuts.

Howler Monkey

Smaller Primates

Lemurs, bush babies, and tarsiers are also primates. Bush babies spend the day resting, high in the African rain forests. At night, they search for food. Their enormous eyes help them to see well in the dark.

Dwarf
Galago

Fast Food

African pottos are related to bush babies. They move very slowly, but make a fast grab at the birds, snails, lizards, and fruit they feed on.

Potto

Meat-eaters

Tarsiers have very long fingers and toes to help them cling onto trees. They are the only entirely meat-eating primates, feeding on insects, lizards, frogs, and birds.

Tarsier

Loudest Monkey

South American howler monkeys are the noisiest monkeys of all. They live in groups of 15 to 20 animals. Howler monkeys often howl in the early morning, before the group sets off to wander through the trees in search of food. They will also howl to warn others off their territory, and their cries can be heard for many miles around.

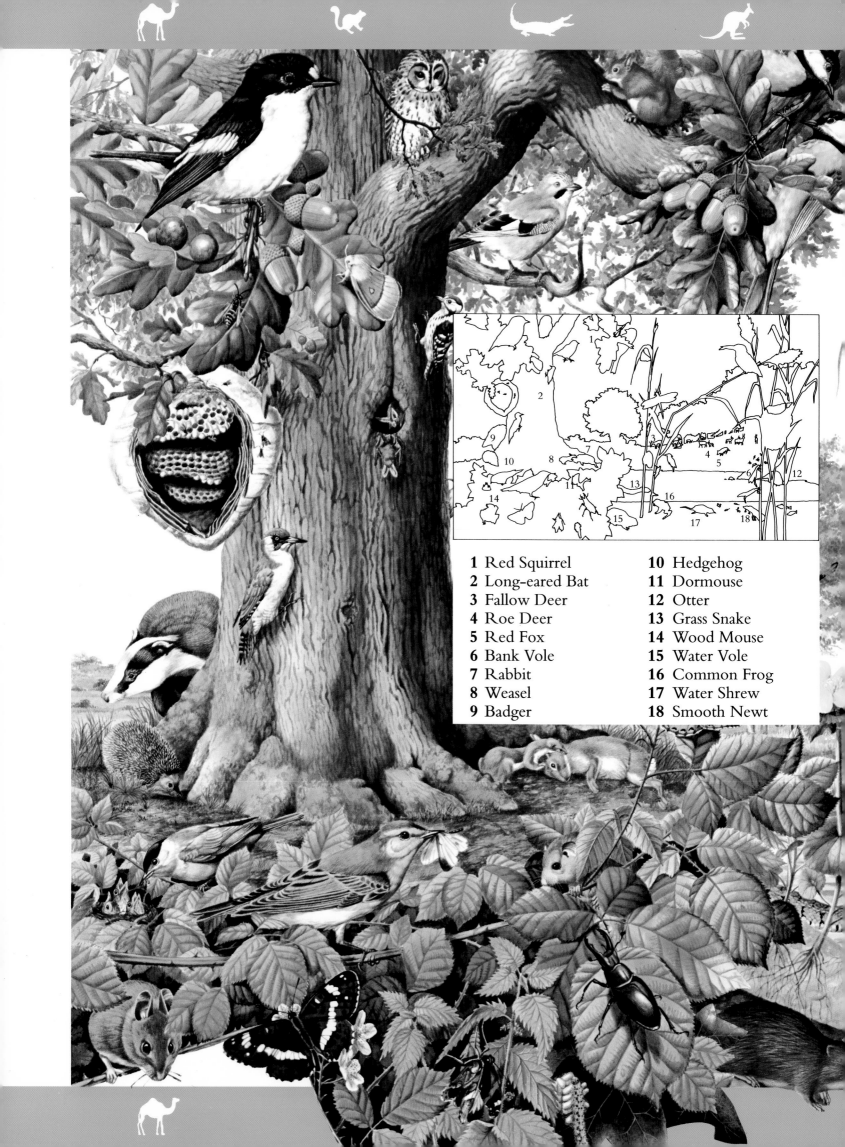

1 Red Squirrel
2 Long-eared Bat
3 Fallow Deer
4 Roe Deer
5 Red Fox
6 Bank Vole
7 Rabbit
8 Weasel
9 Badger

10 Hedgehog
11 Dormouse
12 Otter
13 Grass Snake
14 Wood Mouse
15 Water Vole
16 Common Frog
17 Water Shrew
18 Smooth Newt

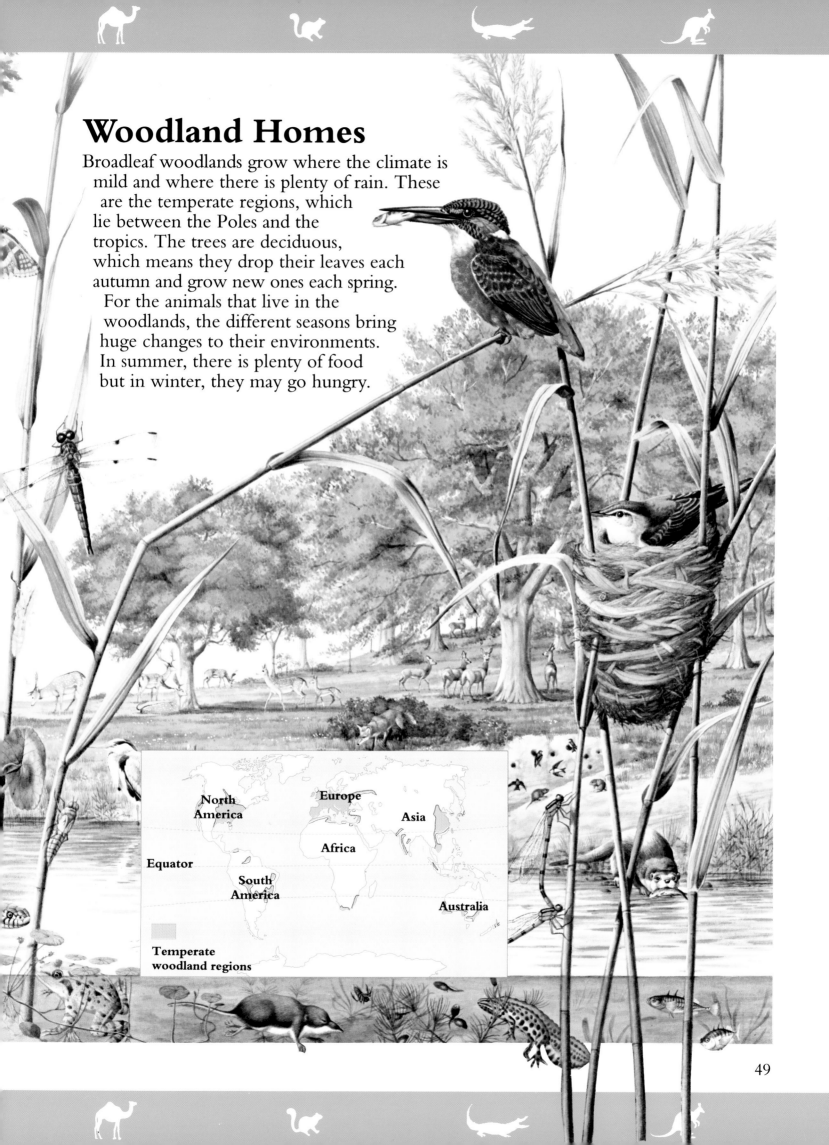

Woodland Homes

Broadleaf woodlands grow where the climate is
  mild and where there is plenty of rain. These
   are the temperate regions, which
lie between the Poles and the
tropics. The trees are deciduous,
which means they drop their leaves each
autumn and grow new ones each spring.
 For the animals that live in the
  woodlands, the different seasons bring
huge changes to their environments.
In summer, there is plenty of food
but in winter, they may go hungry.

North
America

Europe

Asia

Africa

Equator

South
America

Australia

Temperate
woodland regions

Wanderers of the Woods

Most animals that live in the woodlands are small, with the exception of deer. They live on the ground, where they search for food among the leaves and plants. Up in the trees, squirrels build their nests, called dreys.

Predators, such as foxes and weasels, hunt for the plant-eating mammals. Many of the woodland animals make their homes and raise their young in the woods but wander far from them to feed. They visit nearby fields and marshes, and even farmland.

Gray Squirrel

Tree Runner

Gray squirrels make their nests, or dreys, high up in trees. Fearless acrobats, they can leap from branch to branch, and run straight up tree trunks. Gray squirrels feed on nuts, seeds, birds' eggs, and young chicks.

Cunning Carnivore

Foxes are members of the dog family. They can live in all kinds of places, including towns. Foxes hunt at dawn and dusk, and eat a wide range of food, from hares, voles, birds, and insects to fruit and scraps from trash cans. Sometimes, foxes use an unusual trick called "charming" to catch young rabbits. The fox chases its own tail or leaps up and down until the rabbit is fixed in a trance. It then stops dancing and pounces.

Excellent hearing, keen sight, and a good sense of smell make foxes expert hunters.

Red Fox

Fox cubs are all born blind. Their eyes open after about a week.

The long bushy tail is sometimes called a "brush."

Female foxes, called vixens, are smaller than males and do not have a thick ruff of fur around their necks. Devoted mothers, vixens will run any risk and face any danger to protect their young.

Weasel

Ferocious Hunter

Weasels are related to stoats, badgers, skunks, and otters. The smallest members of the family, they are only about 8 in (20 cm) long. They live in European woodlands, where they are ferocious hunters. They will attack birds and animals larger than themselves, biting them in the back of the neck. They more often feed on small rodents, such as voles and mice, and birds' eggs.

Fishers

Raccoons live in the woodlands of North America, usually close to water. They eat almost anything, but their favorite food is freshwater crayfish, a kind of small lobster. They use their front paws to search underwater for the crayfish.

Raccoon

Badger

Underground Homes

Badgers look like small bears but are related to stoats and weasels. They live all over Europe, North America, and China. Badgers feed at night and make their homes in a maze of underground tunnels.

Wildcat

Forest Cat

Wildcats live in the forests of Europe. Their larger American cousins are the bobcats. Wildcats look like domestic cats, but may be over 3 ft (1 m) long and have shorter, thicker tails. They live in dens, or cracks between rocks, and hunt at night for small animals, such as hares and rabbits.

White-tailed Deer

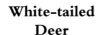

Woodland Deer

North American white-tailed deer were once badly overhunted but are now protected by game-control laws. Their name comes from the long, white, bushy tail. Male deer grow antlers that may be 20 in (50 cm) across.

Rabbit

Danger Signals

European rabbits live in underground tunnels, which they dig with their front paws, kicking away the loose earth with their back legs. They feed only on grass and other plants, often badly damaging tree bark, seedlings, and farm crops. When danger is near, rabbits warn one another by thumping on the ground with their hind feet.

Woodland Facts

The largest areas of deciduous forest are in Europe, the United States, and China. They are also called broadleaf woodlands.

Rabbits have as many as 30 babies in a year and they can do great damage to crops. In the 1950s a disease, called myxomatosis, was introduced into Europe and Australia to control their numbers. Within a few years, the disease had almost wiped out the rabbits but their numbers are growing again.

A Cycle of Seasons

In the temperate woodlands, the weather changes with the seasons. The woodland animals have a yearly cycle of activity that is caused by the conditions. Some animals, such as hedgehogs, survive the cold winter by hibernating in underground burrows. Most animals give birth to their young in spring, when the plants begin to grow. During the summer, there is plenty of food. Autumn is the time to prepare for winter. Animals, such as squirrels, collect a store of nuts and seeds to feed on during the cold months.

European Hedgehog

The Big Sleep

In winter, European hedgehogs hibernate, curled up in a thick nest of leaves and grass. When animals hibernate, their breathing slows right down and their hearts beat very slowly. Their body temperature falls to around 50°F (10°C). The store of fat in their bodies built up during summer and autumn keeps them alive until spring.

Skillful Swimmer

Otters have short thick waterproof fur, webbed feet, and broad, flat tails. Excellent swimmers, they spend most of their lives in the water. They can close up their ears and nostrils when they dive underwater for fish. Otters also feed on shellfish, as well as birds and frogs.

Bank Dwellers

Water voles live in burrows that they dig in grassy banks close to ponds or streams. Sometimes the burrow has one entrance above water and one entrance below. Water voles dive well and are expert underwater swimmers. They often groom their fur after a swim.

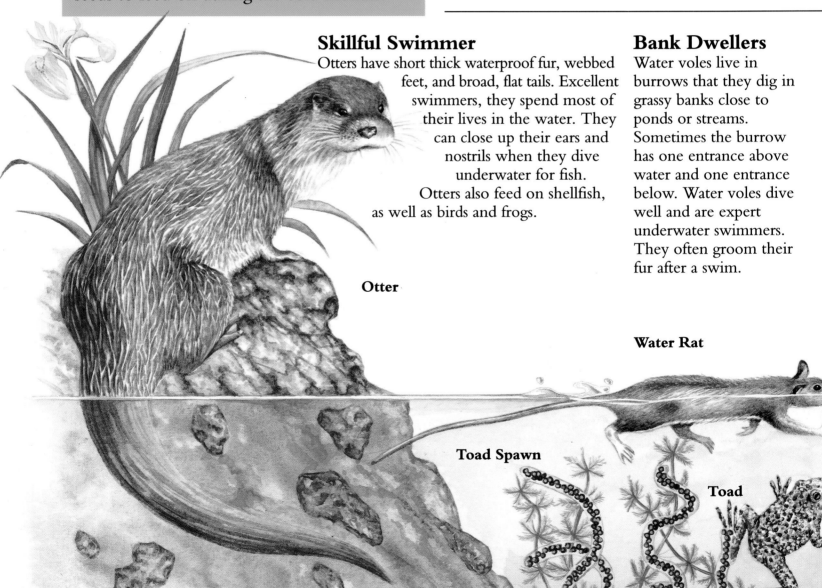

Otter

Water Rat

Toad Spawn

Toad

Dormouse

Sleepy Snake

Adders prey on small reptiles and birds. They hibernate through the winter, waking up in early spring. Adders are poisonous, although their bites very rarely kill people.

Raccoon Dog

Cosy Nests

Tiny common dormice are found in woodlands all over Europe and western Asia. When they hibernate, dormice curl up inside soft, warm nests, with their long tails tucked around them.

Adder

Hibernating Dog

Raccoon dogs feed on small rodents, young birds, insects, and fruit. They are the only members of the dog family to hibernate in winter.

Good Appetite

Tiny water shrews sometimes spring out of the water to snap up insects buzzing above the surface. They also feed on fish and frogs, as well as earthworms. Shrews are big eaters and may chew their way through twice their weight of food each day.

Sticky Eggs

In spring, female smooth newts lay their sticky eggs, one by one, on underwater leaves. They bend the leaves over the eggs with their feet to protect them. About two weeks later, the eggs hatch out into newt tadpoles. By late summer, the young newts will have grown and developed enough to leave the water and live on land.

Fishlike Young

Most frogs and toads must lay their eggs, called spawn, in water. Many travel each spring to the same pond or stretch of water to breed. Frogs lay their spawn in floating, jellylike clumps on the surface of the water. Toads lay their long strings of eggs in deeper water. During the following weeks, the eggs hatch out into tadpoles that slowly change into frogs or toads.

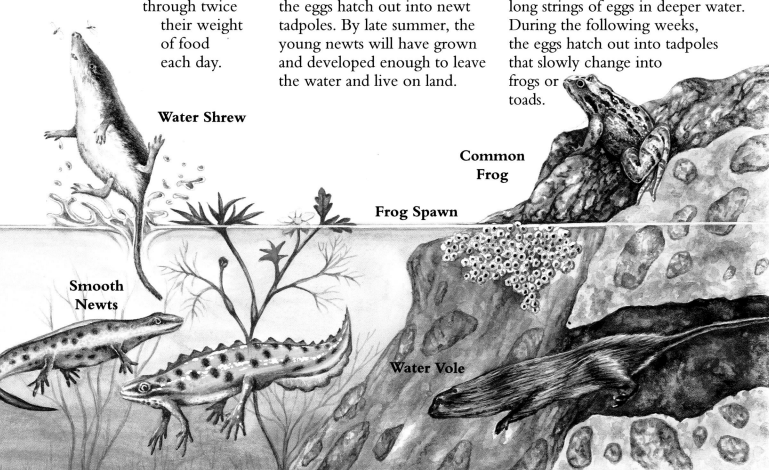

Water Shrew

Common Frog

Frog Spawn

Smooth Newts

Water Vole

Island Oddities

The plants and animals that live on islands are often very unusual. This is because they can change and develop – or evolve – in their own ways, quite separately from those on the mainlands. They may also have different food and conditions. Some island animals are similar to those in other places, but have grown much bigger. Others have become tiny versions of their mainland cousins.

Few animals have been on islands since the islands were first formed. Many arrived long afterward, by flying, swimming, or being swept there by ocean currents and strong winds. Newcomers that live and breed on an island are called colonizers.

Babirusa Pig

Curved Tusks

Babirusa pigs live on Sulawesi, off the coast of Indonesia in Southeast Asia. They have strange, curved tusks that grow up from their lower jaws through their top lips.

Giant Lizard

Komodo dragons, which live on four small islands in Southeast Asia, are the world's biggest lizards. They can grow as long as 10 ft (3 m). Their only enemies are the local people, who hunt the wild pigs and deer that these giant lizards feed on. Komodo dragons are becoming rare and are now protected by law.

Komodo Dragon

After a big meal, Komodo dragons may rest for as long as a week without eating.

Komodo dragons have powerful tails that are useful weapons against attackers.

The people who first saw Komodo dragons thought they were ferocious crocodiles.

The long thin forked tongue is very sensitive.

Saltwater Drinkers

Quokkas live only on one small island, off the coast of Australia. They have to drink salt water because there is no fresh water available.

Quokka

Living Fossil

Tuataras live on rocky islands off the New Zealand coast. They are the last survivors of a group of prehistoric reptiles that lived 140 million years ago.

Tuatara

Tenrec

Many Babies

Many kinds of tenrec live on the African island of Madagascar. Hedgehog tenrecs hold the animal record for the most offspring. These small mammals may have up to 32 babies in one litter.

Giant Tortoise

Sole Survivors

Lemurs are primates, found only on Madagascar and some of the nearby islands. They range in size from tiny mouse lemurs, which are only 5 in (13 cm) long, to sifakas, which can grow to 22 in (55 cm). Lemurs live almost entirely in the trees – only ring-tailed lemurs spend time feeding, playing, or resting on the ground. They are expert climbers and some sifakas can leap enormous distances from tree to tree.

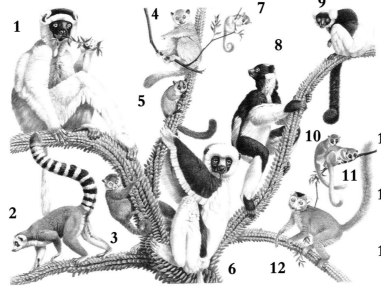

1 Verreaux's Sifaka
2 Ring-tailed Lemur
3 Weasel Lemur
4 Gray-backed Sportive Lemur
5 Fork-marked Dwarf Lemur
6 Coquerel's Sifaka
7 Gray Mouse Lemur
8 Indri
9 Ruffed Lemur
10 Brown Mouse Lemur
11 Fat-tailed Dwarf Lemur
12 Mongoose Lemur

Long-lived Reptile

Giant tortoises live on the Galápagos Islands in the Pacific Ocean, and on Aldabra Island in the Indian Ocean. They can grow to 5 ft (1.5 m) long. Giant tortoises may live to be 100 years old.

Fighting Males

Male land iguanas on the Galápagos Islands have ferocious battles during the mating season. They may bite each other but the fights do not often end in death.

Land Iguana

Island Facts

About two million years ago, there were very small elephants and hippopotamuses living on islands in the Mediterranean Sea.

The new colonizers of an island usually arrive by chance. Insects and birds may visit as they are flying past. Other animals may swim across from land nearby. Some mammals and reptiles reach islands by floating on rafts of vegetation, swept downriver and out into the ocean.

Seaweed-eaters

Marine iguanas spend their days feeding on underwater seaweed along the rocky coast of the Galápagos Islands. At night they climb back on to land to sleep.

Marine Iguana

Australian Mammals

The island continent of Australia was formed about 50 million years ago when it broke away from a much larger piece of land. The plants and animals on the new island were separated, or isolated, from the rest of the world and evolved in their own way.

Australia today has its own unique animal and plant life. Best known are the many kinds of marsupial mammals, only a few of which have survived outside of Australia.

Marsupials

Marsupials are mammals with pouches. At birth, a marsupial baby is not developed enough to be parted from its mother. So it spends its first weeks in its mother's pouch, a kind of pocket, where it feeds on her milk. As the baby grows, it starts to leave the pouch for a short time. Gradually, it spends more and more time out of the pouch, learning to fend for itself.

Kangaroo

Smaller Relative

Wallabies are close relatives of kangaroos, but much smaller. Like kangaroos, they use their strong back legs to hop along at great speed, and balance with their tails.

A kangaroo's short front legs are only used when it is moving slowly or stooping to feed.

Champion Jumpers

Red kangaroos are the largest kangaroos. Males may be 6 ft (2 m) tall. They can hop very fast over short distances, reaching speeds of up to 25 mph (40 kph).

Koala Bear

Wallaby

Eucalyptus Diet

Koalas are small, bearlike marsupials. The name "koala" is an aboriginal word, meaning "the animal that does not drink." Koalas eat nothing but the leaves of eucalyptus trees, which give them the food and drink they need.

A long, strong tail helps them balance.

Powerful back legs help male red kangaroos jump as far as 30 ft (9 m). They are also useful weapons against attackers.

Tiger Cat

Climbing Cat

Tiger cats are the largest of Australia's marsupial cats. They may be over 3 ft (1 m) long. Tiger cats are good at climbing, extremely strong, and very fierce. They prey on birds, as well as small wallabies and rodents.

Tasmanian Devil

Roomy Burrows

Wombats dig large, long burrows underground to escape from the heat in the day and the cold at night, and to hide from predators. These marsupials have teeth that grow all their lives and are worn down by chewing.

Wombat

Greedy Scavenger

Rare Tasmanian devils are found only in the forest and scrubland of Tasmania. They prey on a variety of animals and are also greedy scavengers, gulping down the remains of dead animals.

Sugar Glider

Tree Glider

Sugar gliders live in Australia's coastal forests. A type of possum, they are both expert climbers and skilled gliders. By holding out the webs of skin between their legs, and using their tails to help them turn, they can "fly" from tree to tree. Sugar gliders feed on the nectar, sap, and buds of flowering trees and hunt for small insects under the bark.

Egg-laying Mammals

Platypuses and echidnas are two of the oldest and most primitive of mammals. They are the only mammals that lay eggs. Platypuses, which live in southeastern Australia and Tasmania, may grow to about 2 ft (60 cm) long. They spend most of their lives in water, using their ducklike bills to catch worms and crayfish. A platypus's bill is soft and rubbery and very sensitive.

Echidna

Egg Layer

A female echidna, or spiny anteater, keeps her one egg in a special pouch. The egg hatches after about ten days, and the young echidna stays in the pouch until it is ten weeks old. By then, its growing spines make it uncomfortable for the mother to carry.

Platypus

Animals in Danger

All animals need the right conditions to stay alive. They need food and shelter, and they need to breed. The conditions are so bad for some kinds of animals that they may not be able to survive for much longer. These animals are called endangered species.

Many animals are in danger because people kill them for their meat, skins, horns, or tusks, or because they invade farmland and eat the crops. They also die when their natural habitats are cleared for farming or for building, or when pollution prevents them from breeding and rearing their young.

Valuable Wool

Huge herds of vicuñas lived in the high Andes of South America. They were killed for their valuable wool, considered to be the best in the world. By 1970, only a few thousand were left.

Vicuña

Kouprey

Kouprey

This wild ox lives in the forests of Cambodia in Southeast Asia. Very little is known about it. In 1969, there may have been 100 koupreys. By now they may be extinct.

Starving

This solenodon lives on the island of Cuba in the Caribbean. It is starving to death because mongooses were brought to live in its habitat and are eating its food supply.

Cuban Solenodon

Black-footed Ferret

Plowed to Death

Plowing the North American prairies for crops and building is destroying the black-footed ferret's home and its food, the prairie dog.

Tiger

African Elephant

Land Giants

African elephants are the largest living land mammals. They once lived in most of Africa but were killed for their tusks. Now they live mainly in reserves in central Africa.

Beautiful Coats

Tigers are now threatened because their jungle homes have been cut down and they have been hunted for their beautiful coats.

Tropical Rain Forests

Huge areas of rain forest are cut down every year for timber, for farm and building land, and to make roads. This destroys the homes and food of animals, endangering their lives. Without help, many may soon be extinct.

Because of this threat, the number of woolly spider monkeys in Brazil has dropped to a few hundred. Rare lion-tailed macaques of India are also affected by forest clearance. Macaques will not cross open land. Some groups live cut off in very small areas of forest. Unless they can meet other groups, the macaques will be unable to breed healthy babies.

Lion-tailed Macaque

**Woolly
Spider Monkey**

Javan Rhino

These small rhinoceroses once lived in the thick forests of Indonesia. Today, there are only about 50. Although they are now protected, they are still hunted by poachers and killed for their horns.

Javan Rhinoceros

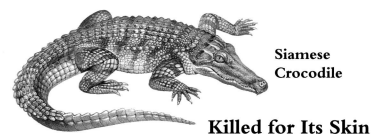

**Siamese
Crocodile**

Killed for Its Skin

The Siamese crocodile is now almost extinct. It survives on a crocodile farm in Thailand. All species of wild alligator and crocodile are endangered by hunting for their skins.

Bechstein's Bat

This bat lives in Europe but is becoming rare as forests and woods are destroyed. It is also being poisoned by pesticides.

Bechstein's Bat

Red Wolf

Hunted

Red wolves once roamed all over the southern United States. By 1970, very few were left, except in zoos.

Mount Nimba Toad

The Mount Nimba toad of West Africa is one of the few toads that gives birth to live babies.

Mount Nimba Toad

Onager

Onager

The growing herds of domestic grazing animals have left little food for wild onagers. They survive in the driest parts of Iran where there is very little food.

Protected

The rare Spanish lynx is one of the most endangered animals. There are only about 1,500 of them left. Almost all of those live in a protected nature reserve, the Coto Doñana in Spain.

**Spanish
Lynx**

Endangered Animal Facts

In China, 12 reserves have been set up in the bamboo forests to protect rare giant pandas.

Unless people act now to save them, experts say that 50,000 different kinds of animals will die out in the next 50 years.

Reserves have been set up in India to save tigers and encourage them to breed.

In South America, vicuñas are protected in nature reserves and their numbers are now beginning to increase.

Zoos and Wildlife Reserves

The first zoos were places where people went to stare at animals that were often in tiny cages. Today, zoos still entertain people but they also preserve animals, sometimes breeding them so they can be returned to the wild where they have died out.

Game parks and wildlife reserves are home to many animals. Here they live in their natural habitats. Some reserves have been set up to study and protect wildlife, including animals that are in danger of dying out.

Saved from Extinction

Some very rare animals have been saved from extinction by zoos. Przewalski's horse, the only living wild horse, once roamed the Asian steppes but was wiped out. Now over 500 horses live in zoos.

In 1972, the last herd of Arabian oryx was shot. A small herd lived in the Phoenix Zoo in Arizona. In the 1980s, groups of oryx born there were released back into the wild.

Arabian Oryx

Przewalski's Horse

Chimpanzee

Chimpanzees love playing and climbing. In zoos, they need ropes to swing on, climbing frames, and other toys.

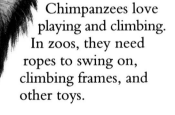

Park and Reserve Facts

Each year, huge areas of rain forest in South America are cut down and cleared. Now, the National Amazonia Park protects a region where animals such as anteaters, monkeys, armadillos, and tree frogs can live in safety.

Black rhinos were once found over most of Africa. They were hunted for their horns until they were almost wiped out. Now, most black rhinos live in parks and reserves but only a few thousand of them are left.

Bored Animals

Some animals do not live happily in captivity. Polar bears and big cats such as leopards, which live alone in the wild, suffer when they are kept close to other animals. Animals that live in groups, and are very active in the wild searching for food, become bored and lonely when they are kept in bare pens. Some of them develop strange behavior.

Reptiles in Zoos

Alligators, crocodiles, snakes, and lizards must be warm to be active. Most zoos have reptile houses, which are kept at 79° to 85°F (26° to 29°C). Round Island boas are the rarest snakes in the world. In 1985, babies hatched in a zoo for the first time.

Round Island Boa

Happy in Zoos

Good zoos and wildlife reserves keep animals in family groups and try to give them the space and kind of environment that is as close as possible to their natural habitat. Plant-eating animals that live in groups, such as deer, spend most of their time feeding and live happily in captivity. Meerkats are small mongooses. They are burrowing animals that live in southern Africa. They live contentedly in zoos in family groups. In one Australian zoo, the chimps live in a big grassy field with trees, rocks, and a stream. They live and play here almost as they would in the wild.

Breeding Rare Animals

A zoo's most important job is to conserve, or keep safe, rare animals. One way to do this is by helping them breed.

Some animals, such as lions, baboons, and deer, breed easily in captivity but others never produce young. Zoos carry out research to find the best conditions for the different animals.

Gorillas do not breed well. In 1961, the first male gorilla to be bred in a zoo was born in Switzerland.

Gorilla and baby

Giraffes have been kept in zoos for many years. They are gentle and are not afraid of people. They breed well in captivity.

Giraffe

Reserves and National Parks

The first game reserves were set up as hunting grounds. Today, they are areas where animals are protected by law but poaching is a problem in many reserves. North American wood bison were thought to be extinct until 1957, when a herd of about 200 were found in a Canadian national park.

Wood Bison

Home Comforts

Rhino enclosures in zoos may not look comfortable. But in the wild, these animals walk on hard ground and wallow in muddy pools, so zoos aim to provide similar conditions.

Glossary

Amphibian Cold-blooded animals that can live both in water and on land.

Antarctic Area around the South Pole. Also called Antarctica.

Arctic Area around the North Pole.

Canopy The roof-like cover made by the tree-tops in a forest or wood.

Carnivore An animal that eats other animals.

Climate The type of weather a region usually has.

Cold-blooded An animal whose body temperature rises or falls with the temperature of its surroundings.

Colonizer An animal which moves to live and breed in a new place.

Coniferous A tree, usually with needle-like leaves, which keeps them all the year around.

Crustacean An animal with a hard shell and soft body, such as a crab.

Deciduous A tree that loses its leaves at the end of the Summer.

Environment The surroundings in which an animal lives.

Evolve To change and develop slowly, over thousands of years.

Extinct An animal species that has died out and there are none still alive, is said to be extinct.

Habitat The natural place where an animal or plant usually lives.

Herbivore An animal which eats only plants.

Hibernation A long, deep sleep, or time of little activity, during cold or heat, or when there is no food.

Invertebrate An animal without a backbone, such as worms, insects.

Mammal Warm-blooded animals which usually have hair or fur, and feed their young on milk.

Marsupial A mammal whose young are not fully formed when born and grow in their mother's pouch.

Migration A regular journey made by animals, often at a certain season, to avoid a cold winter, a drought, to find food, or to breed.

Mollusc An animal with a soft body and often a shell, such as a snail.

Nocturnal Active at night.

Omnivore An animal that eats both plants and animals.

Pampas The grasslands of South America.

Poles The most northerly and southerly, and the two coldest, places on Earth.

Prairie The grasslands of North America.

Predator An animal which kills other animals for food.

Prey An animal which is killed by another for food.

Primate A group of mammals that includes apes and human beings.

Primitive An early form of plant or animal.

Rain forest A dense forest of tall trees found in tropical regions.

Reptile One of the main groups of vertebrates. Reptiles are cold-blooded animals with scaly skins, such as crocodiles and snakes.

Rodent A small, gnawing mammal whose front teeth keep growing.

Savanna The grasslands of Africa.

Scavenger An animal which eats dead animals or plants, or the remains of another animal's kill.

Species One type of animal.

Steppe The grasslands of Europe and Asia.

Taiga Coniferous forests stretching across northern Europe and Asia.

Temperate A region with a mild climate.

Tropical A region with a hot, rainy climate all the year.

Tundra Frozen land between the North Pole and northern forests.

Vertebrate An animal with a backbone.

Warm-blooded An animal whose body stays at the same temperature, even in hot or cold weather.

Index